Advice to Single Women

Advice to Single Women

Haydn Brown

The British Library

First published in 1899 by James Bowden

This edition published in 2015 by
The British Library
96 Euston Road
London NW1 2DB

British Library Cataloguing in Publication Data
A catalogue record for this book is available
from the British Library

ISBN 978 0 7123 5781 4

Cover by Rawshock Design
Printed in Hong Kong by Great Wall
Printing Co. Ltd

Contents

ADVICE TO SINGLE WOMEN

INTRODUCTORY

WOMEN are the offspring - bearing members of humanity, and it is scarcely possible to make a study of their health, real or ideal, without bearing very strongly in mind this their peculiar mission. It would be possible to refer to the health of single women as one might treat that of young men, the same treatise indeed answering for both, but the value of such a work could only be very poor in comparison with one that bears strongly in mind, throughout, this delicate, hidden, mysterious, sanctified, and supremely important aim and end of woman's existence. The health of man is one thing, and is sufficiently serious a matter to dwell upon in volumes, but it is even more necessary to be anxious about, to be solicitous for, and to be industrious

ADVICE TO SINGLE WOMEN

over that of woman. Is she not the
gentler, the fairer, the weaker, and by
nature the more timid and retiring? Is
she not the "better half" of the pair
"whom God hath joined"?

After close observation of the lives of
both sexes, one is almost bound to come
to the conclusion that men take care of
their health better than women do. This
is no doubt partly due to the necessity
they understand for keeping themselves in
bodily and mental fitness for the arduous
tasks that constitute their daily employment; but it is also largely influenced by
the fact that it is easier for men to look
after themselves than it is for women, in
various ways and for several reasons.

A man is supposed to keep himself up
to some masculine degree of health and
strength; it is more or less a disgrace to
him as a male member of society if he do
not. But women can be anything as long
as beautiful, and sometimes useful, in a
womanly way: this at any rate seems to
be the rough idea prevailing amongst very
many of both sexes. On the one hand
it is a disgrace if a man have not a
healthy countenance and is not in due
season sunburnt; but it is generally preferable for a woman to be pale-faced, if
her beauty is increased by it, no matter

8

whether she be healthy or not. Some women seem quite prepared to take the risk of being ill as long as there is a fair chance of earning a good complexion by some means. In other words, health and strength are man's chief points of beauty —or handsomeness, if any one should not like the former word; while delicacy of structure, softness, and a pale-peachy appearance are amongst the most admirable attributes of women. The reader will see at a glance what influence this great difference of appearance and build is likely to have on the proportion of ill-health between the sexes; the one has a natural and instinctive inducement to maintain sound health; the other has just the opposite.

This picture is presented in rather a harsh and pronounced light, perhaps; but main points like those advanced are very difficult to impress unless they are marked out quite clear and with some emphasis. In treating of subjects like the present, the simple rule had better be given in its fulness and entirety, and then exceptions may be brought out of various kinds to prove it. To give an ordinary instance of the latter, many men see the greatest beauty in *health* and not in the sickliness of women; though these are men who know that a consumptive countenance may be surpassingly beautiful if not too far affected with the disease, but that it must be at the same time very unstable and argue extremely unpleasant promises for life and joy in the future. Therefore the idea of beauty in such a case as this is governed largely by a calculation on health as well. It will, however, be seen in a later chapter that, generally speaking, a young woman's health is the very last thing thought about by an admirer of the opposite sex. She is pale but pretty ; she has charming manners ; she carries herself in a stately way ; she is entrancingly feminine ; she is everything, in short, that simply overwhelms a man, with her innumerable and inexplicable fascinations, and she forbids any thought whatsoever on his part that is likely to interfere with a certain, undivided, complete, and everlasting possession of her ; everything else, even the very vital point of health itself, is allowed no place in the lover's thoughts at the stage of following or wooing.

But should women not attend to their health as much as men? Why certainly they should! They have a right to possess just as good health, and perhaps better, taking some circumstances into account. There are all reasons, except perhaps that of fashion, why women should be muscular, active, and healthy-looking, and as strong—in proportion, of course—as men. All women would be healthier and none the less beautiful if they possessed firm muscles and strong limbs; this scarcely any one could controvert. Some might be found to argue that it is not in the least *necessary* for women to be strong, that they are just as well without good muscles provided they are shapely, and that strength is rather dangerous to beauty; but a greater mistake could not be made. A pale and fine complexion might be, in a sense, beautiful, and it may be rare; but it certainly could not be the most desirable to those who have sufficient brain and thinking powers to enable them to discern disease under its surface.

If women would only look a little into the future, and bear in mind that the powdered face of the bride they are looking at, as she walks along the path of the churchyard that leads to her carriage again, is merely a show that will be rubbed out of countenance, or, if they would take the warning that something more than a pale and captivating countenance will possibly be discovered during a honeymoon, they would get well on the way to learning the uselessness of "marvellous" complexions, considering them things of the surface, and further seek to become acquainted with such methods of general improvement to health and appearance that if studied and worked upon would give more satisfactory and lasting causes for admiration.

And if a girl never intends to marry she should be none the less mindful of her health. Good health during young days not only means brightness and pleasure then, but it lays the foundation for happiness and contentment in the future. Old maids are not given credit for having the very best of tempers on all occasions, but nothing would help them to maintain an even-minded satisfaction concerning their lot, in the face of those all-absorbing duties that attend the happy life of their more fortunate and twice-blessed sisters who are wives and mothers, than health of body and mind.

One must be quite fair to the gentler sex, notwithstanding, and bear in mind that there are certain differences in temperament, brain, and nerves that make women less fitted and inclined for health—and muscle-seeking than men. There is some amount of excuse for ill-health and flabbiness to be found in natural disposition alone, no doubt. Men are by nature so constituted that they are eminently fitted for fighting and all the varied activities of contest, and consequently health and strength is theirs, a good deal without their thinking about it, so to speak. Women undoubtedly have the harder task before them in looking to their health. They naturally lack the combative spirit of the sterner sex ; while their mind, which has never, in former generations at any rate, been trained up to so high a pitch, is often less resolute and determined. A natural nervousness and timidity will also contribute very largely to any other hampering to which their endeavours and actions may be subjected.

Suppose we compare the average health of young unmarried women with that of men of a similar age. We shall find them far more neuralgic, far more back-aching, ever so much more headachey, certainly more irregular in bodily functions ; more listless and lifeless ; more requiring the doctor. They are placed under the bane of constipation, for instance, to an enormous degree. They suffer very commonly from anæmias, of a kind and severity that man knows practically nothing of. They are liable to a set of complaints quite peculiar to their sex, to which nothing can be found corresponding fairly in the male.

It is not for a moment argued that men are rarely unhealthy; they have their complaints badly enough, in all truth. But the fact is nevertheless urged upon the reader that a fair balance is not to be found, by any means, between the sufferings of men and women, no matter what period of life may be studied, or whether under single or married conditions.

It might be interesting at this stage to compare roughly the anatomy of man and woman, and by such means show how the latter is physically and physiologically handicapped in the race for health and strength. Men are usually bigger-framed and stronger-boned than women. Their muscles have also greater power, not only when specially developed, but in a natural and untrained state. The bony attachments of muscles as well as joints and ligaments of the male are coarser and firmer. Man seems to have been made for fighting and feats of endurance, while the fashioning of woman has been on lines that agree with a quieter, less aggressive, and more passive temperament. The haunch-bones of man were designed for strength, while those of a woman were largely intended for a body that has to undergo certain changes and experiences attending child-birth.

The general circumstances under which the majority of young women live render them likely to fall behind men in general health. Man's employment leads him more out of doors, and is more muscle-exercising than is that of the greater number of woman-kind, whose duties are largely domestic or sedentary, or of the shop-assistant kind. Your men labourers are out-door individuals; your women workers of a similar class are either sitting factory-hands or domestic servants. Gentlemen of position are travellers abroad, hunters, sports-men, farmers, yachtsmen, polo-players, who, when still younger, went in for boxing, rowing, fencing, football, cricket, and so on. Ladies of the same class drive in the park, take afternoon tea, do shopping, read novels, parade in dress, attend concerts, and engage in needlework, for the most part. Of course there are exceptions: the habits of the two sexes are broadly contrasted for purposes of rough illustration. Certainly some ladies hunt, fish, shoot, play cricket and golf; some even fence and box; but not any of these things are cultivated to the extent they are by men. It must also be confessed that there is an increasing tendency for ladies of the higher classes to engage in manly occupations, and to divert themselves with such heavier exercises, at the present day, that would not have been thought of in years gone by : still, there are yet very great differences between the habits and actions of the two sexes, though even now we are threatened by a third sex : there are "higher women," "advanced women," "pioneers," and such like, cropping up as quite a distinct set, shaping themselves as well as they can into something between men and women.

The difficulties of finding the proper means of procuring health and strength for women are real ; they are so because until comparatively recently, and then only to a certain extent, it has not been considered at all necessary for girls to engage in physical exercises with any distinct object. Many things have militated against women's chances of ascending, or of even safely holding their own. In the first place there have been considerations of decorum to hamper choice. It is not even now considered fit for women to do all in the way of sports or athletics that men do, in our present way of deliberating. We may all some day think no more of the sex in bloomers giving high kicks at football than we do now of cycling skirts and golf-playing, and then we may see girls' football matches

played as often as we do men's, and for
every male gymnasium a female one also.
But that day will scarcely arrive yet.

Having gained some idea of the small
amount of exercise and fresh air that the
working classes of women, in shops,
factories, and service, are able to obtain,
it will readily be seen that in order to
counteract so large an amount of inactivity,
nothing short of daily systematic use of
muscles and limbs by some of the definite
and fixed ways to be found under direction
and regulation in institutions and clubs
would be of much avail. And it may well
be supposed that a long time will have to
elapse before such advantages are reached.

As regards exercise for girls of a school
age, much the same complaint as runs
through some of the foregoing paragraphs
may be made. School-girls have not the
amount and variety of exercise that boys
have, and there are not the same opportunities given them for it. A girl who was
invalided home from a boarding-school
was once asked by the writer what the girls
of her school did out of school hours, for it
was supposed from the appearance of this
particular one that the life led was not a
particularly healthy one. Her reply was,
after some thought and hesitation, "We
either read or quarrel." This spoke

volumes. There was really nothing to induce them to do anything else; three-quarters of an hour's walk, in crocodile order, with measured step and slow, was all these poor things got in the way of exercise each day. No wonder they quarrelled; and if they fought one need not be surprised, for that is what any beings caged-up are very much inclined to do when they can find no other use for their stiffened limbs. A school where girls quarrel much is bound to be one in which very little outdoor exercise and amusement are provided. Things are getting better every day, it is true; but it will be a long time before as much is done to provide exercise and healthy diversion for girls at school as there is for boys. And, with hard school-work, girls want it, surely! It is all very well to argue that it is not necessary for girls; this bald reasoning will not do. Fresh air and exercise are quite as important for the one as the other.

Perhaps it would to some extent encourage young women to make a study of their health if they were assured that though pale faces and small waists are marks of beauty sometimes, so are healthy cheeks and moderate waists in their way. Things that women imagine to be beautiful are not always so accepted by men. It is more the *general* effect that men note. So many women pin their faith to one, or perhaps two, points of beauty—take their teeth and waist, for example—and they pay so much attention to the one or both that everything else is forgotten. Movements, or set of the head, erectness of figure, proper position of the shoulders, grace of gait, becoming arrangement of the hair—all these may be thought nothing of through the entire attention being rivetted to something else that may happen to strike the idea or fancy for the time being. The result is that either the general effect, which, to repeat, is really what men notice, is not favourable, or still worse, the concentration of the ideas on one thing makes the *ensemble* of the girl quite ridiculous. Some girls have been known to put on a stupid expression of face just in order to show what they know to be a pretty set of teeth. Men have wondered what they have been grinning at, and could not understand why there has been such a peculiar fixed set of the head, until it has dawned upon them that the girl they are noticing prides herself and pins every bit of her faith on her teeth—as Katisha of the "Mikado" thought she wanted nothing more than an elbow.

Others there are who have conceived

the idea that small waists are the be-all
and end-all of beauty, and they have even
been mad enough to try to reduce themselves by sleeping in very tight corsets.
The consequence of such a foolish idea has
been this : the general health has suffered
under this one-sided notion, and all other
points of attractiveness have gone down
just as the waist has. Some have nipped
until they have reddened their nose ; this
result they have deserved. In not a few
instances the nipping of waists has simply
resulted in the nippers being very much
stared at, not admiringly, by men, be it
understood, but with astonishment and
disgust of their own sex. And what has
been the general effect ? The aspirant to
waspishness has brought on a stiff and
stupid walk, without proper movement or
grace of turning, and an appearance of
being afraid of stooping or laughing for
fear of bursting something or breaking in
two. Then the sighs that are heard ! And
the fear of taking food !

No ; health is much more beautiful, if
women would but believe it. Do not the
classic statues of Venus prove it ? A
moderately small waist is what should be
desired—something between a man's and
a modiste's.

The great question of what employments

are suitable for girls is one that cannot be too well studied. This advice may be given : women should engage in whatever employments they are able, whether these should belong to the male sex or not, provided such are reasonably appropriate, in most respects, to their own sex. The more remunerative the better ; but the more healthy the nature of them the better still. The kind of work that necessitates very many hours' sitting should be avoided if possible. It is certainly difficult to pick and choose in these days of so much competition and small wages ; but this book will not have been written in vain if girls may be induced to take into account the question of health more than they do when they think of earning their own living, and to appreciate this fact, that, of all things they may earn or possess, good health is after all the most valuable ; without it, nobody is well-off, nobody is really beautiful.

ADVICE TO SINGLE WOMEN

THE HABITS AND CUSTOMS OF THE TWO SEXES COMPARED

WOMEN very often remark that they wish men had to "go through" what they do. It will appear at times that the sufferings they have to undergo are entirely unbalanced by anything that the male has to endure. But the habits and customs of the two sexes are so very different, and the capabilities, structure, and energy so essentially laid on different lines, that comparison seems almost absurd. Both are human, and this is about all one can say with any safety.

It is with a view to studying the question whether an average woman's life is the best one to lead, taking into account her great mission in life, reproduction, that the idea of contrasting her mode of living with that of man takes root. Suppose we ask ourselves this question: If man had a feminine abdomen would he be more suitably constituted to bear children than a woman? The reply must be, Yes and No.

ADVICE TO SINGLE WOMEN

In strength and powers of endurance, in firmness of mind and force of determination, he would. But he would fall very short in womanly and motherly tenderness, and in that very feminine attribute—a simple, uncomplaining, and contented long-suffering.

So that after a rough analysis of constitution and temperament in the two sexes it seems that the only thing women want to make them perfect as wives and mothers is the physical strength of men in proportion. This is a point I would like to see red-lettered. The chief habits and customs that obtain amongst men and women render the former as near as possible perfect for the aims and common duties they have in existence, while the latter have great imperfections in development and structure, considering the severe and exacting part they have to play, not quite so constantly, it is true, as seen in the exertions and works of man, but certainly occasionally and sometimes often. It is this latter fact that provides the foundation of the discrepancy in physical fitness that is complained of. If women were to be constantly employed in a manner that made them strong and muscular, as men are, then we should no doubt see a great difference in capacities and fitness during the days when they travailed or were heavy-laden.

ADVICE TO SINGLE WOMEN

To all intents and purposes the male and female of all wild animals are built as to their muscular development more or less equally. For instance a tiger and tigress are equally well physically equipped, in proportion to their size and form of frame, for running, leaping, or hunting prey. Similarly the female of the horse, dog, or any other animal is suitably built and perfected. In some instances the male amongst animals will be found to be the bigger, and in others, much rarer, the female; but the muscular development of each, leaving out of account simple size, will invariably be found proportionally equal. It is equal because the habits of the two sexes are about equal. It cannot be denied that the male of most animals is the more aggressive and ferocious, while he will more successfully war against enemies than the female; yet the female can be strong and ferocious when she likes, as when tending young, showing she is physically fit when opportunity occurs. The point, then, that requires emphasis is this, that all things considered, the muscular development and proportional power of the female of animals is equal to that of their male representatives.

When we turn our attention to animals that are kept under domestication we see quite a different state of things. We meet the veterinary surgeon before we have gone many yards. From him we gain particulars of hitches and complications that attend the advent of progeny, when breeding comes under the direction and influence of man. This class of animal may be said to occupy a position about half-way between human beings and wild animals, as regards their physical and constitutional fitness ; they are generally more physically fit than the former but nothing like so perfect as the latter. Their work is irregular and varied, and perhaps not so good for them as the instinctive or voluntary kind prescribed by nature, and their food is more or less artificial or selected for them by their keepers. As a result, their muscles and general health are not so good as may be found in their wild relatives. The tone of their health is not quite so vigorous. Even cows suffer from consumption, when kept in a domesticated state, as is well known ; and it will be admitted that any living thing that is consumptive will have a poor chance of going through the labour of producing offspring.

As a whole, therefore, domesticated animals are not so unfit for producing offspring in an uncomplicated and natural way as women are, because they are better developed, and still further because a certain artificial selection of them is found expedient. They are better developed because they are mainly kept as beasts of work or burden, and a certain muscular energy is required of them, and they are " selected " for the same reason.

It is an instructive fact that the greatest amount of complication and disaster connected with labour amongst animals is to be found in that class which most resembles women in certain particular respects. Those domesticated specimens that take the least exercise, that are the most confined indoors under more or less imperfect hygienic conditions, are the ones to go wrong in their confinement, namely, milch cows. Now, this is not a treatise on natural history, it is not a book on domestic economy ; but this much is sought, that the reader shall, by simple observation and common comparison, gain some true and accurate idea of what is and what ought to be, in respect to her most sacred and serious function.

It should follow quite clearly from the above that the less women are domesticated the better they will be fitted to bear children. Well, yes, this is one way of putting it. But points of practicability and human convenience and decency have to be taken into account, notwithstanding. No one by a thought can add one cubit to his stature; and it would be no use laying down the law once for all that women, to be the best of all women, should be men as far as ever they can, that they should mould themselves after him in mind and matter to the very last point. The change would not be easily effected, however much women desired or men admired; for we know that many things make women and various thoughts sway men.

Yet we have an interesting example of a certain tendency to shifting of the sexes, so to speak, that has arisen in the ordinary evolution of men and things. Has not a section of women broken loose from skirts and conventionality, in order to prospect for the golden chances of manhood? Have they not made a bold dash for two legs and liberty? But, before leaping, these daring damsels have not looked on the other side, however, or they would have seen their Klondyke without its nuggets; they would have found the mines "salted" and not sound, and realised themselves sexed without the seed. They leapt, and stood on the other side a picture judged by many more hideous than before. No; ladies, clubs and bloomers, of themselves, will not raise faulty humanity.

Now we are able to reduce our reasoning

to a much simpler sum. A proper amount of exercise of the right kind, and taken regularly from childhood up, is what will help to make healthier girls, better wives, and more perfect mothers. Some of the lessons given by nature should be taken as indications of what is right and wrong, what is favourable to wifehood, and what is prejudicial to posterity. Girls should be provided with opportunities of taking wholesome physical exercise at schools or institutions, and it should seem as necessary to bring up girls with good chests and well-shaped limbs as it is for boys. Girls are full of sport, though boys do not seem to think so; they only want fair opportunity. A movement in the right direction has certainly been apparent during the last few years: girls play hockey a good deal now, and an immense number engage in tennis, golf, and cycling. Gymnastic exercises have also found fair favour, and swimming is much more common amongst girls than it used to be.

Still, there are two sides of the question. Just as men cannot afford to allow athletics and gymnastics to interfere with the stern duties of wage-earning, so young women should certainly not be encouraged to follow the same kind of diversions to the exclusion of either their own wage-earning duties—if they have to work for a living—or a judicious amount of domestic training, if they look forward to becoming wives. Let women sail as near to men as possible in the battle for *health*, provided their amusements are reasonably decorous and suitable to the sex ; but the progression very far into man's habits and tendencies that such seeking might involve, should not lead them to neglect or minimise all the best and most beautiful attributes of their sex. They should not seek too eagerly and hastily after bifurcated garments and shirt-fronts, for apparel alone will not indicate the way to become healthy, and still remain women.

However, everything that is best is arrived at by means of the marked boundaries and lessons of extremes, in nearly almost everything. A government and opposition is good, because after contest we are able to find something between the two that is the most advantageous for a people's general advancement. So "higher women" take a beneficial and salutary departure from the ordinary, when they array themselves in battle against their lower sisters, in spite of men, and leave a victorious product in the centre of the fray, a derivative manifesting sweet reasonableness, a conquering cohort that has also learnt a lesson.

ADVICE TO SINGLE WOMEN

The lower examples of womankind have a chance of learning many things from the higher. They may be roused to the thinking point, to say the least, by some dress that causes their simple eyes to stare and their mouth to open, or by some action that might only be calculated by the more cultured to amaze a mere animal understanding. Even so far, so good; for, with the little training and opportunity that many women have, there is scarcely enough in them to think at all deeply. There are men also who do not think, my sisters, but not so many, because by circumstances they are more forced.

The "higher," or "advanced," examples of women will also learn many things from the lower. They will find that notwithstanding their bloomers and cigarettes, whether in clubs or on the turf, they are nevertheless always anatomically similar to their quieter sisters. And, moreover, even development of muscle itself availeth nothing like so much if a pretence of spinsterhood or barrenness is passed by fate. An "advanced" woman may argue and stamp her foot at the inequalities of the sexes, but she will not fail, sooner or later, to find something admirable in wifehood; she is certain to see some exposition of the blessings of motherhood at one time or another. Let her scorn the mere man as she may, and make a bold attempt to ride heavyshod over him, she must allow him the powerful prerogative peculiar to him as her sexed opposite; she will proceed to very ridiculous and impossible extremes if she attempt to do more than imitate his clothing, copy his gestures, study his habits, and have a great deal to say about unfairness.

One word more : there are innumerable things that "higher women" can go in for, and even beat men in, about the propriety or advantages of which there might be much difference of opinion; but let them never lose sight of their health if they ever think of the holy state of matrimony. In regard to this prospect they may have three things, Faith, Hope, and Health; but the greatest of these is Health.

TIGHT-LACING

MY readers have a right to know as much of their anatomical arrangements as will make them appreciate the fact that their chest contains lungs for breathing, and these are encased in what doctors call the walls of the thorax, understood by everyone as the chest walls. The latter are formed of bones, namely, the front chest-bone, the spinal column between the shoulder blades, and ribs that spring from the spine. The interval between each rib is filled up by muscles that are required for the expansion and contraction of the chest. The ribs are attached at one end to the spine, and curving round the sides, they end in front at the chest-bone, or in cartilage that is firmly united to bone, excepting the two lowest on each side, called floating ribs; these are not attached to any bone in front but are fixed as the others are to the spine behind.

The upper set of all these ribs, having attachments in front and behind which are not fixed but jointed and movable, are all capable of movement up and down, as they must do on breathing. It is true they are helped in their action by other muscular systems that are to be found in the body, but that need not trouble us at the moment. It is quite sufficient to understand that all the ribs move, and why they move. Any external pressure will have the least effect on the upper ribs, attached as they are to bone at both ends. The lower ones are much more compressible, because their anterior attachments are only soft and cartilaginous — while the lowest two on each side have even no attachment at all in front. It is necessary to note these points, because tight-lacing involves the lowest ribs chiefly, and the others only partly.

A shrewd woman once argued that because the lowest ribs, those that are so pressed upon when a waist is nipped, are not fixed in front, this must have been a provision of Nature designed in order that waists should be contracted; but she was wrong, however, for Nature never intended that women's waists should be like wasps'. Nature wished, when she sanctioned the making of woman, that her chest should rise and fall with perfect freedom, so that good and easy breathing might take place, in order to keep the body properly alive. The very working of the ribs, so beautifully on their bony attachments, under muscular action, dictates an injunction against the wearing of anything that should impede it. If ribs were made to move for a distinct and vital purpose, and, notwithstanding, are deliberately bound and fastened down, is it not likely that something will go wrong?

It must be remembered that only the more advanced races, those most civilised, have taken to tight-lacing. Fancy this! The more we know, the bigger fools we of humanity seem to be, in some things. Even savages allow full freedom to the movements of the chest, and would not think of hindering their breathing by tying something tight round the waist, not they. Aboriginal blacks will cut themselves about the face and body, will pierce themselves with rings and all sorts of cruel instruments, but they could never think of strangling either their waists or their necks while they had their senses. Hence we find that such low-down specimens of humanity as these are able both to breathe well and to move with ease and grace.

Suppose we look at the orign of tight-lacing. As everything feminine came in due course to be considered beautiful, or something to be admired, waists were

marked out as a special point for judgment.
Men were considered judges first, and
women afterwards—men on account of the
admiration they were able to bestow, as
opposite-sexed beings, but women largely
on account of envy—and women very soon
find out what men admire — hence the
development of nipping.

The Chinese also nip, but not waists;
they go in for feet. Their ideas about
waists are just the very opposite to those
of Europeans. Chinese ladies leave their
waists absolutely free; but, my word! they
put all their energies into making small
feet. It may well be thought which is the
worst thing to do, to nip waists or feet.
Both are bad enough, and so the question
had better remain unanswered; though,
probably, the waist-nippers would get the
palm for wickedness from an impartial
judge. For the bones are only doubled
up if a foot is bound down, and walking is
only hindered; but the poor, panting lungs
required for breathing and simple living
are cruelly treated and threatened when
the chest is forcibly ensheathed.

Let us have small waists by all means, as
many as woman-kind can provide us with;
but not the artificial article, please. There
is everything that is lithe and dainty,
something femininely fetching, about a

pretty little waist; but when it is fashioned with such difficulty, and under so much agony, one loses interest in it to a great extent—it is not the real article, so to speak. Of course, girls think that no one can tell the difference; but they are mistaken. The difference can be seen even at a distance sometimes, but it may also be detected at close quarters by certain signs and symptoms, the chief of these arising from this law: that one point of feminine beauty is rarely cultivated to a great extent without the effect being seen on other points. And it is these other effects that are often first noticed: such as a peculiar walk, a stiffness of gait, a hesitation to bend or move, a disinclination to eat or hurry, and so on.

No; we want naturally small waists, as many and tiny as women can let us have. Men would not cry out so much against artificially-made small waists if they did not know what patience and suffering were spent over them, and if they did not see so well the other marked defects caused by them. It is the harm that is done, against the very little amount of good, that causes comment.

There is no doubt whatever that artificially-small waists are very much admired by a few, or are at any rate particularly noticed; but the reader had better know at once that, as often as not, a nipped waist is marked as one of the insignia of points of character about the person cultivating it. Almost every one knows how to read a painted face; some will translate it one way, and some another, but it is generally fairly well understood by the majority of men who know anything. And so a nipped waist has its meaning: it argues corresponding general anxieties and great efforts to please; it denotes the exercising of both true and false attributes for the envy of the one or for the edification of the other sex. It spells much looking-glass practice and astonishing bills.

Now, what are the symptoms of tight-lacing? Those who nip know them well enough, but those who do not will notice in others not only a small number of inches, according to the calculation of the eye, but a cased sort of rigidity all around, and the parts just above the constriction will lack that freedom of movement—very, very slight—that should be seen in walking—only trifling in amount, though just the little that ought to be there—enough to show a free and natural spinal action. Then again, if the breathing be observed it will be found rather short and cramped, and very often varied and irregular, now and then only a laboured sigh. Sufferers will also be seen to turn very pale occasionally; and a general unhealthy look will not uncommonly help to draw the casual observer's particular attention to them. They will often refuse to eat for no apparent or explicable reason, and they are given to suddenly retiring from company, but withal returning soon, trying to look as if nothing had happened. Bad digestion, and a good deal of pain in front of the waist, is frequently experienced.

What actually takes place, therefore, in tight-lacing is this: the lower portion of the chest has its expansive action bound down, while the ribs, that should be quite free, are forced inwards, with the result that breathing is seriously impeded, and, at the same time there is such pressure exerted on the stomach that it is sometimes found to be hour-glass-shaped. The action of the heart and large blood-vessels is sometimes interfered with also, and an improper circulation is produced, which may be noticed in the hands, feet, and sometimes head. The nose may even turn red, especially if, in addition, dyspepsia be present to help it.

The following case serves very well to illustrate some of the effects of tight-lacing; it also shows how certain symptoms may be entirely mistaken and possibly lead to quite tragic *dénouements*. At the dining-table of a fashionable foreign hotel a rather attractive-looking girl used to seat herself daily during the season, always in the same place. She was a good deal noticed by most of those near enough on both sides of the table; but nearly opposite her sat a good-looking, sunburnt fellow, whose letters used to arrive addressed Captain something-or-other. Now it was one of the most natural things in the world that these two should notice one another—in fact a sort of Marconi *rapport* was created at once, and an unwired and noiseless telegraphy established that transmitted slight sensations even to those quite near. Others certainly began to notice the influences at work. Perhaps only a pretended *insouciant* turn of the head, or a glance towards the other end of the room, would be given by one or the other; but this was quite well enough seen, even though the face of the interested observer might be apparently directed towards a soup-plate. They went on, until the officer could not help humorously turning in his mind, as he took up the menu-card, such ideas as might be expressed in this manner: "What else is there to come? Ah! Five good courses and sweetmeats: yes; . . .

39

more like a lot of nonsense and eye-making; for that girl there has no appetite, evidently, and I can never do justice to a dinner when I know someone is carefully counting the drops from my moustache." . . . All near enough were now interested; and the various glances and little symptoms that were shown during meal times formed the subject of lively chatter amongst young and old for some twenty minutes afterwards each day.

The girl was attractive, because of her general appearance; and she also had an especially small waist; not made by Nature alone, but one of those that take a considerable amount of time and trouble to get to perfection—the kind that is arrived at by degrees, after much patience and concentration of effort. Her whole hopes, her sole calculations, were now centred on her waist. She imagined, of course, that this was what *he* was looking at, and what every one was admiring; this was, doubtless, what all the other girls at the table so envied Our aspirant to captimonial honours nipped, and nipped again, the more they stared each day. She heaved sigh after sigh at the table; ate mere crumbs, and would not stoop in the slightest degree, not even for soup. "She is in love now, no doubt about it," an old lady said in the drawing-room,

most of the others quite agreeing with her.
"And how she shows it! Fancy anyone
sighing like that at a dinner-table; . . . and
eating nothing! How stupid lovers are, to
be sure!" The Captain thought so too,
and no mistake: he knew the symptoms
well enough.

While all this kind of thing went on
developing, my lady never lost count of
her waist: "Whatever may come of it,"
she said to herself when she returned to her
bedroom for a few minutes' breath, " I do
get some admiration, not only from him
but from the whole table. They *do* stare :
it is *rare* fun. Dinners I like ; but attention
I could not exist without. That woman on
the left would give her right hand for such
a waist as mine : and that fellow there, he
does look." Each meal time the whole
scene was enacted, with little variation,
except that now and again the girl turned
quite pale, and once or twice left the table
before any of the others. This was all put
down, however, to the agonies and trying
turns incidental to suppressed, separated,
and silent wooing. But a particularly careful
observer would have perceived more pale-
ness than blushing, for the *affaire du cœur*
to be a genuine and altogether true one.

One day, however, the whole table was
startled, and every appetite annihilated, by

a frightful scream coming from that pedestal of beauty, the seat usually occupied by my lady of fashion, the pale and pretty little martyr : she had gone down in the grip of suffocation and fainting. The visitors flew right and left ; down the corridors and to the hotel entrance ; whistles brought cabmen ; some yelled " A doctor : fetch a doctor ! " others burst into the secretary's office and urged on repeated telephonic messages. All was confusion. Even the Captain himself thought he had experienced nothing like it since his last scramble for revolvers and safety at the frontier when the card-party—which he will never forget —was surprised by the enemy at dead of night.

A doctor came, and the girl was removed to her room. For some days the awful truth did not leak out : only guarded bulletins were issued, until it was announced that the patient had been ordered away, even without permission to say good-bye. Then particulars were freely given out. A servant had overheard the nurses talking to one another, and she had gleaned the information that " the doctor said she had barely escaped with her life : it was all her corsets : she was nipped until the skin was nearly broken."

There was not very much love or longing

connected with all her sighing and pining after all : it was only really tight-lacing that affected her in this way.

Another lesson may be learned from this case : after all the girl's efforts, the good-looking man of the piece was the least moved of the two, from beginning to end. Even a captain is not always to be caught by a corset, it seems, unless, perchance, it should be his own—and captains do wear them sometimes.

Perhaps young women would like to know how the generality of men estimate them : it is always so nice to get to know *really* what others' notions are and how to arrive at them. Well, they are more widely comprehensive in their calculations than is commonly supposed : they do not admire any one particular thing about a woman. One of the greatest mistakes of all that girls make is this :[1] that any one point, or perhaps two, makes them. One sees this delusion at every turn. The things men take into account are *general* appearance and effect, not particular ties or trimmings.

[1] And by girls is meant, of course, single women generally, for two spare spinsters of upwards of fifty were once heard to make pointed reference to themselves and their afternoon with the remark, "We giddy girls have been to Earl's Court."

ADVICE TO SINGLE WOMEN

Sometimes a fellow will be talking to a girl about someone else "who was there," and all at once the latter will say, "What did she wear?" showing that she thought that what was worn was enough for anyone to go by, and was the only thing of importance that a man would regard. "The apparel oft proclaims" the woman, in the eye of woman, no doubt, but it is a fact, nevertheless, that the details of a woman's clothing are the very last points that a man takes notice of. He *may* notice something very startling, but it is the general effect that he pictures. He might possibly notice a waist with other characteristics, but he knows that a waist cannot make a woman any more than a head of hair can make a face. Generally, when a girl cultivates one thing in particular, this is not very much noticed by others, because it is so hidden amongst the other peculiarities of appearance or walk that are present on account of this one thing. For instance, there is no doubt whatever that Englishmen notice the very peculiar strut that Frenchwomen display, long before they see the high heels that cause it.

If one were to ask the average man what he meant by a "nice girl" he would not explain that she had a sixteen-inch waist and wore mauve ribbon in her hat: he would be more likely to reply that she had taking manners, that she walked in a fascinating way, that her voice was lovely, that her figure was most pleasing, that—that—he could not say exactly what it was about her, and so on. Men do not fall in love with a tiny waist, unless the owner happens to have several other points of beauty to carry it off. The human male likes proportion and artistic beauty, with ease and grace of movement, and all bound together not by a corset but by ineffable charm of manner.

Corsets or supports are often necessary ; of course they are. Many figures require them, and some would be no shape at all without. But they should be reasonably adjusted, to serve legitimate ends. It is the duty of everyone, young and old, to study their appearance to some extent. Simple artistic feeling and common education or culture command it. Appearances that are much neglected, and which denote indifference and idleness as regards right and judicious care in mode of living, are revolting and offensive to the sensitive perception of those who are honest-minded, sensible, and healthy-souled. Yet, on the other hand, to cultivate artifice to excess and injure the health at the same time is maniacal and nothing else.

ADVICE TO SINGLE WOMEN

The following case mentioned in the present author's book, "The Secret of Long Life," is interesting, as showing the evil effects of tight-lacing :—

"Dr George Danford Thomas, Coroner for Central London, held an inquest at the Islington Coroner's Court respecting the death of D—— B——, aged twenty-two years, lately residing at 3, S—— Road, S——. Deceased, a domestic servant out of a situation, went to Northumberland Avenue for the purpose of witnessing the motor-car procession. When in the crowd she told a friend that she felt stifling and ready to faint. They went to Trafalgar Square, where her friend left her. About midnight she returned home, and complained of being unwell. The next day she put her feet in mustard and water. Shortly afterwards she was found stooping over the bath, and she fell in a fit and became insensible. It was then found that her corset was very tightly-laced. Before a medical man arrived the deceased expired. Dr John Smith, of Stapylton Hall Road, stated that he had made a post-mortem examination of the body of the deceased, and found that death was due to syncope from heart disease. The deceased was a stout woman, and there was no doubt but what stooping over the hot water, and her being so tightly-laced had caused the attack of syncope and death. The jury returned a verdict in accordance with the medical evidence.''

Would it be safe to give an account of how tight-lacing is carried out? Scarcely. It *might* teach some young women who are yet innocent. But, however, on second thoughts, the innocence concerning such matters must be so rare that perhaps very little harm will be done; and, moreover, there may be some methods that only a few know of, which, by their very barbarous nature and the amount of discomfort and suffering they cause, will be fought shy of, by the majority certainly; so, taking all things into account, perhaps some slight benefits may be conferred by a little exposure.

There are certain girls who put themselves in training, as it were, for a small waist. They will eat certain kinds of food, and very little of it. Then at certain times of the day they will have a good squeeze; such discomfort could not be borne for long at first; it would not do to put on the screw at all times yet; several spells of rest are necessary. Measurements are taken at frequent intervals during the course of treatment, and the closest comparison is made with the progress of others who may also be in training, or who may be taking finishing lessons. There is a great deal of altering and sewing going on at the same time, remember, to make things fit, and the aspirant to wasp-waist honour must not be disappointed at bursts and breaks-out for some little time. New corsets will be wanted also, according to the fancy, whether for mere narrowing purposes or because of the general contour of the *corsage* that is aimed at and appears to be *de rigueur*.

Various kinds of help are often brought into requisition; binding, tying, wringing, pulling, and tugging are all done in their turn. And the aid of others is of course very valuable, now and then. A friend standing on each side to pull or compress, push or wrench, will help very considerably; and bosom friends well remember the copy-book heading of their school-days, " Do unto others," &c. They are quite willing. Leather belts are good helps for training, as one would imagine; they can be put on almost next the skin if necessary, so that something loose may be worn outside; by this means the nipping will be less apparent, and the chances of bursting the clothing reduced to a minimum.

Those who have got desperate have even been known to sleep in their corset, or with something very tight round the waist. It is not at all necessary for any reader to get cross with their sex on learning of such an advanced and wicked procedure; this would do no good whatever; the simple truth must be taken calmly and sensibly.

Quite enough has been given in the preceding paragraphs to convince the thoughtful reader of the foolishness and danger of tight-lacing; while an attempt has been made to show that there are other things to be admired besides small waists, and that the latter are by no means everything to be desired, for more reasons than one.

A marked characteristic about women who nip is this: they will never own it. They will gesticulate, and go into a temper, and expostulate with proffered proofs that " such is not the case," to such an extent that *their nipping may often be known by the manner in which they will retaliate upon an accusation*. The girl who does not nip does not get cross when accused; if her observer be of the same sex, she will merely reply, " Don't be jealous," and will then laugh. But some nip and really think they do not; they imagine that so many others nip very much more and they do not count their own worth speaking of.

ADVICE TO SINGLE WOMEN

Occasionally one can find extremely small waists which are naturally so and have never been subject to inordinate pressure of any kind. Happy are they who have them. But their jealous sisters of fashion will not believe them, if they deny that they tight-lace, unless they have indisputable proof of it. Those who really nip will never believe that others exist who do not. They are certain that nearly all nip, but that only some can be as successful as they themselves are.

Wise mothers sometimes exercise a watchful eye over the waists of their daughters. Now and then this detective work is over-practised, however, and there is a tendency to attribute every pain and sigh, every pallor and blush, to tight-lacing. The case is remembered of a mother accusing her daughter, who had been taken with some slight indisposition, of nipping. The doctor was called in. "Will you kindly speak seriously to her, doctor," the peremptory parent began; "she draws in her waist too much, that is what is the matter with her; it is nothing else." This was the drift of the argument before the daughter was present. When the latter made her appearance it was evident that at that moment there was as much mental trouble as bodily illness, for the girl's eyes were red and swollen and she had evidently been crying a good deal. Without giving time for questioning, she at once burst out, " Mother says I have my belt too tight, and it is a mistake, I have not." It is quite true that the measurement was very small to all appearance ; and considering the importance of settling the question definitely, in order to quell an obviously unhappy feeling that had existed between the two for some time—to set all minds at rest if possible— it was deemed advisable to test the effect of the belt the girl was then wearing, as well as her corsets. By this means any wrong impression would be dispelled, and a more correct diagnosis of her case rendered possible. It was found on examination that no undue pressure was being exerted at the waist. The patient had gone down considerably in weight recently, without doubt, but she had not shown it much in the face, however. Everyone at once rejoiced at the glad news, tears dried up quickly, and happiness once more reigned throughout the house.

For the detection of tight-lacing, therefore, symptoms are of much greater value than ocular or palpable proof ; cases have been known where patients have " dressed for the occasion" and have gone on nipping again afterwards.

In a former chapter stress has been laid on the importance of exercise, if young women wish to be healthy and have hopes of one day becoming happy mothers. Now it is quite obvious that all exercises of any value must have free and well-formed waists for the performance of them. What can a girl do in a tight corset? And it is not sufficient for her to leave this painful figure-former off merely when she is going to play golf or hockey. Her waist must not be too bound up at any time, because it will not gain its proper muscular development if a certain amount of freedom is not allowed at all times. Any part of the body that has its movements limited, in whatever way, will be deficient in its muscular power. So a nipped waist will be found to be weak when loosened only occasionally for sport or games.

Just a little consolation, and an exposure of men, and we have done with this subject. Who would ever have thought that a brisk business is being done in men's corsets at a certain address in the West End of London? Yes, they do; men wear corsets! that is, some do. What a sign of unsexed stupidity, to be sure! With all their faults and failings over dress, men love women still, and can make a good deal of allowance when sitting in judgment over their pretty but often naughty little ways with their waists. But for a man to nip!—Words entirely fail. A "third sex" made out of women, indeed! What about these new men? A "third sex" of *men*! It would seem that the very best thing for both these new products would be to sentence them to marry one another; and so, force them, unsexed as they both are, to work out their extermination, in the punishment meted out to them of having to endure their own close society. They really deserve one another.

A DELICATE SUBJECT

A MOMENT'S consideration will show that while men need have no scruples about seeking advice concerning their ailments, large and small, women have a good deal of reason for thinking twice: the gentler sex is by nature more retiring and shy, and prone to endure the pangs and punishments of illness with a silent and long-suffering contentment. So much do they themselves realise this that they are in the habit of laughing at the pains of men.

"A man cannot bear the smallest pain," is a very common saying amongst women; and, certainly, a good many instances occur to prove the truth of it. It is quite true that men are often great cowards in the presence of accident or bloodshed; sometimes absurdly so. The case may be related, by way of example, of a butcher who once had his fingers crushed in a sausage-machine. His mate brought him at once for surgical treatment. There being comparatively little pain, on account of numbness, it was decided that the ends should be trimmed up without the man being put under chloroform. He was placed in a chair, and his friend in need ordered to stand behind him to hold his hand up firmly and steadily. While arranging instruments, solutions, and stitches, it was seen that the amateur-assistant butcher, a big burly man, was sinking down behind the chair in a dead faint. A draught was soon given him, and a peremptory reproof as well, when he recovered sufficiently— not through pure want of sympathy, it must be confessed, but in order that the man might be spurred on, as it were, to do his duty at an awkward juncture; for now was not the time to show any weakness of heart—at any rate this was the natural sentiment of a doctor under the circumstances, whatever others might think. The operation was concluded after a good deal of trouble, the greater part of which was created by the fainting assistant. The most curious part of the story is to come. On dressing the wound the next day, it was remarked to the patient that his mate was worse than he himself was through the operation ! Whereupon the laconic answer came forth, " Yes, sir; and the funny part of it is that he was killin' sheep all the morning."

It is also very true that women sometimes bear pain badly, and that they often cannot witness sights of blood without showing signs of fainting. But many such cases are directly dependent on the state of health. People, both male and female, can endure less of anything that troubles or worries when their general health is not good. And, so many women are not in a good state of health, by reason of their work or confined habits, that it is not to be wondered at if we find faint-hearted ones to be far from rare.

However, apart from the question of human endurance of painful and sickening sights, women are by nature so constituted, and their relationship with the opposite sex is such, that a good deal of hesitation will be shown amongst them before they complain of their own bodily sufferings. They have not such a bold front as their masculine representatives of the race. The same is seen amongst animals. The male generally presents by far the boldest and strongest presence in the face of attack or danger. It cannot be denied that the female of them is also very ferocious at times, when she is engaged in the tendance of her offspring, for instance, as has been elsewhere mentioned. But, broadly comparing them, the male is the master of most situations. Notwithstanding all these comparisons, the female of both animals and human beings is by nature more retiring when anything that appertains particularly to her sex is troubling her. It is hard to go against nature, and in the subject under consideration a very good example of the power of nature is to be seen. Hence no apology will be given for another reference to this almighty teacher's lessons, as they may be learned in the animal world.

Anything sexual is in a sense offensive. A study of instinct will prove this. The tendency to retire is natural in human and animal conduct, when anything is to be performed that involves an action of private organs. The lowest forms of humanity—savages who are little better than animals—learn to gird themselves about with leaves of trees and with grass, and to act with some degree of decency.

But it is quite a mistake to suppose that woman's retiring and reticent nature is exhibited in the presence, and on account, of man only ; it is also seen very largely in front of her own sex, even. It is no doubt true that the most perfect and the fullest sympathy is to be found between those that are opposite-sexed. Yet women can sympathise with women enough in cases that men do not understand, and where it is not desirable that men should know anything about the matter. In such instances women can show the highest sympathy, if they like. But taking everything into account, opposite-sexed sympathy is the strongest, when suitable opportunities present themselves for an exhibition of it. The firmest reticence is occasionally shown by a woman before her own sex: some women get very impatient with the illnesses of others of their sex, and often taunt them unmercifully for complaining.

No; women often suffer a very great deal and get little sympathy for it from anyone: thousands there are who would bear out the writer in this statement. The result of all this is, that the earlier stages of diseases, and those little ailments that lead to greater ones, are neglected, and the last state of those sufferers is worse than the first.

Now what is to be done to remedy this state of affairs? Two things. First, young women should learn somehow or other, by books, experience, or observation, that to neglect disease is to create more. Secondly, they should appreciate the fact that, though they may get very little sympathy from either the other sex or their own, there is no excuse for not taking their complaint boldly and sensibly to that quarter made for them, namely, their doctor. And, that they may better see the force of this advice, they are once for all informed that they will not purchase mere sympathy by so doing, even if they get it; they will pay for common duties to be performed. Common duties? Yes, and more — highly-cultured, specially-trained, skilful, and humane treatment. After all, what advantages women have if they would only take them promptly and soon enough! Moreover, for the fastidious and—it would be too severe to say *insanely* sensitive — extraordinarily sensitive, are there not lady doctors?

Knowledge concerning the mistake of waiting too long—or regarding the danger of neglect to complain in the right quarter —and painful object-lessons derived from such delay or error—these constitute the material from which the final adjurations of this chapter are evolved and written down.

ADVICE TO SINGLE WOMEN

SOME IMPORTANT POINTS TO CONSIDER BEFORE MARRIAGE

THOUGH very few who get married have ever thought over beforehand whether they ought or not; though most weddings take place because couples have found, as time went on, that they were so associated with one another, so blended in character and contemplation, after their own ideas, and welded in pure sentiment and indescribable attraction to such a degree, that to have the knot tied would give the easiest and pleasantest way out of what others might judge was promising to develop into a certain and lasting predicament, there are still a few who really do take the trouble to think, who count the cost and weigh the consequences. Fortunate are the few. The step is a most serious one: what could be more so? Boys and girls grow up to an age when they may leave father and mother and go out into the world to do as they please;

they acquire freedom—after much teaching of parents and guardians, and moulded with some amount of discipline—to run their head into a bush of thorns if they should be foolish enough. And they may win a " Dunmow flitch " or handcuffs, an earthly paradise or a life of misery and retribution.

And what does this freedom from parental control permit ? It leads to such attractions and associations of sex as overwhelm the youngster, and apron-strings have not long been cut before a web of heart-searchings and longings is woven around, confusing, distracting, and binding up all aims and inclinations to an exciting and maddening extent. The young woman is not long falling in love ; and before she has even slightly tasted the severities of a cruelly competitive existence she " is over head and ears " into something that at a too early age could scarcely be other than misunderstood, and which has every chance of being very detrimental. And it is hard enough to divine a remedy. To *think* of the probable incidents and consequences of marriage—why, the idea is absurd at this early age ! Previous to twenty, say, few young people ever think of marriage unless they are already overflowing with the desires of love to an extent that they are incapable of all contemplation and calculation : they are carried clean off their legs into church, so to speak.

Marriage before the age of twenty-five is generally nothing more or less than a way out of some love situation that is pulling, tearing, trying, and wrestling with the more important of a person's attributes and attainments. It is not at this early stage of life a well-thought-out and deliberately designed procedure, as it might be and sometimes is at a later stage. Hence the innumerable mistakes that are made. Marriage is like dipping into the "lucky bag"; all parties to the game bring out something, but only a few get hold of packets that are worth much to them. And this must of necessity be so to a very great extent; for experience is the only safe teacher of wisdom, and marriage takes place in ninety-nine times out of every hundred before the one lover knows any more than a quarter of the really-true character or all-round and deep qualities of the other.

Why is it that engaged couples can only know a fourth of one another? For two great reasons and some other small ones. Firstly, they are scarcely old enough to know very much of anything at the age a large number of marriages are contracted; and secondly, the days of their billing, cooing, sighing, and longing are the very blindest and stupidest of the whole of their existence. A man, especially, is never such a fool as when engaged to be married. This is not pessimistic, ill-tempered, or biassed; it is a positive fact. If a man were to go on in the silly manner that he does when in love, in any other pursuit in life, he would certainly be looked upon as an idiot; but, for all that, no blame can really be attached to him; he cannot help it, poor chap. Therefore one can easily see, that, beyond the estimation of mere appearance, which of course is got up to the very last point, and, outside the calculation and prospecting of all the pretty winsome ways and attentions of love-making, it is quite impossible for the one to know the other any more than about a fourth, before marriage.

Young people marry on mere chance very largely, and wait for time to reveal themselves to one another. It could scarcely be otherwise, one must admit. The writer finds no fault with the system; and will not even suggest another in its place. One must simply face the truth as cheerfully and resignedly as possible; these things are what they are, and there cannot be much harm in discussing them, while perhaps a few may learn a useful lesson.

ADVICE TO SINGLE WOMEN

Whether certain people should marry or not depends upon so many things that it would be almost hopeless to attempt to answer the question. As before stated, the final step is generally taken regardlessly, whether or no, and certain important points of suitability are not in the least considered ; in fact, any idea of glaring unsuitability is very often simply kicked overboard on its very first appearance. It is a fact that there are few things which will hasten on marriage quicker than the opposition of relatives or friends who present opinions of an unsuitability order. Some examples are at the moment remembered. A girl was once approached by a senior relative in order that the "real truth about the man" she was engaged to should be revealed to her. A whole list of damning offences of a dreadful nature was dealt out to her, and she was terrorised with all the blackest accounts of his character imaginable. She simply replied, "You can tell me what you like ; if you were able to multiply your charges by two I should stick to him all the more." They were married soon afterwards. Another girl was told that her lover was consumptive and could not live very long after marriage, if he lived until then. She saw herself that this was likely, but in reply to the friends who mentioned the matter to her she said, " If he is only to live a few weeks, and will be happier for it, I shall marry him." After this, why argue?

Reckoning the failures, and summing up the ridiculous circumstances under which many alliances are made, even taking into account the small percentage of real and lasting happiness that is to be found amongst all the married existences one could inquire into, marriage is good. The majority of human beings should enter into the state of Holy Matrimony at some time of their life. The advice may be given to every reader, Marry well if you can ; but satisfactorily at least. And why? Ah! there are some very good and important, not to say interesting, reasons. In the first place, because the intercourse between the sexes in married life is best, most propitious, most complete, and most promising for the future of the race, being, as it is, exclusive and regulated by the bonds of religion and custom ; not promiscuous and deviating, not varied and risky, not wayward and wanton, but right and orderly. Secondly, because a married life conduces to such correctness of living as tends to improve and steady the general conduct. Thirdly, because the life is a quiet and healthy one, calculated to keep down such disorders of action and manner as are prejudicial and imperfect. Fourthly, sexual indulgences are, under marriage association, kept down to a reasonable and harmless minimum, because of the remarkable and peculiar provision of Nature which renders all things that are unvarying less sensuously attractive and enticing than those that present differences. Fifthly, for comfort's sake, and perhaps also for economy's : though there will always be some who squander riches and cease not, who marry and make rash expenditures on the strength of it ? And lastly, marriage succeeds in either raising or lowering, cutting-down or elevating, stirring-up or smoothing-over, the various phases of character and disposition in both man and woman, in a manner that tends to produce such perfection of blend as can only be attained by the union of hearts that are commonly diversely constituted but withal synchronously beating.

The apparent hopelessness of a system of selection—for the regulation of whatever love affairs are ultimately to develop into marriage—generally so well seen when the circumstances of meeting and eventual attachment have been analysed in a large number of instances, would almost make it absurd to study the question of what alliances are most likely to turn out happy and satisfactory ones. As hopeless as it may appear to answer the question, and at the risk of making what may be an entirely useless attempt, let us thoughtfully face the problem.

In the first place, at what age should people marry? Here we are at once confronted with the fact that no two people are alike, and therefore no hard and fast answer can be given to this question. It is quite clear, however, that marriage should not take place until physical development is far enough advanced ; about this there can be no reasonable doubt. From twenty-one to twenty-five years is a favourable age, for then the bones of the body are full grown and well set ; and in addition to the important qualification of physical fitness, a woman's mind is more mature, and her abilities and common sense will have reached a usefully-trained pitch by this time. If she marry young, before her body be properly developed, there would be the danger of an abnormal child-birth. In such a case the result might be serious, and even fatal. Epileptic fits are caused through similar conditions; and such visitations, coming upon the ill-formed and debilitated wife (because of being over-burdened), at the birth, when she is the least able to bear them, imperil a life, or rather lives.

Much under twenty-one, marriages are contracted with an appalling indifference to, and ignorance of, anything and everything, excepting personal and quite superficial attractiveness. Such alliances are bound to turn out unsatisfactory very often. The contract under these circumstances has been signed in the dark. But light cometh at length, when a little older ; and woe betide those couples who find one another very different from what they pictured formerly. There may be much mixed misery for them in the future.

It should be well understood that there are exceptions in the matter of age. Some women develop surprisingly early, both in mind and body ; and on the other hand there are those who ever seem to be very young for their age.

As regards the important question of temperament or disposition, who can know what such qualities are until sometimes long after marriage ? Yet, of course, a good deal concerning character may be gauged beforehand in some instances. Naturally, the best and most favourable temperament for a woman to have is a pure and simple womanly one. This appears to be rather a watery piece of

advice at first sight; but there is a good
deal in it when one comes to think. If
a woman begin to "wear trousers," as the
disposition has been described, that is,
if she begin to take upon herself some of
the duties and directions that properly
belong to her husband, soon after marriage,
there will be ructions without a doubt.
There is a certain sphere in which it is
natural, becoming, and admirable for a
woman to work and have her being; but
let her take upon herself too much of her
spouse's concerns and moods, that only
rightly and properly belong to him as a
man, then she runs the risk of developing
distinct unloveliness in his eyes, at once,
and creates occasions for "words." The
very unhappy life of a personally well-
known couple is called to mind at this
moment: the wife is constantly interfering
in matters which she does not altogether
understand and running against her
husband's work with observations and
aggravating proposals of her own—well
meant but stupidly and hastily thrust
forward — and the result is frequent
discord.

A woman should sharply outline from
the beginning those duties, actions, and
ideas that are purely masculine, and that
should form the right prerogative, so to

speak, of her husband, when she enters the married state. She may all at once, on returning from a honeymoon, feel herself to have a considerable amount of power and authority, in virtue of her "better-half" partnership; but if she wield this carelessly and in glass-houses, a day of "scenes" and glaziers may come. Generally speaking, the husband has the master mind when subjects of wide involvement and of business difficulty present themselves; he has gained it to some extent, of course, while engaged in bread-winning pursuits from youth up; and therefore opposition, when offered by his wife, though possibly well-meant, should be considerately and sensibly guarded. Certainly, there are times and occasions where the opinion or reproof of a wife may be valuable and even well deserved; for it seems almost natural for some husbands to err: a wife has been a pillar of strength to many a weak husband—weak, not necessarily in things that belong to his trained and practised calling, but in matters that are entirely outside of it, such as habits during leisure hours. There are plenty of husbands who are clever in their business or profession, and idiots, or even like madmen (it may be very occasionally, or every time they have the chance, as the case may be) the moment they leave it.

Instances where the wife is distinctly superior to the husband in most matters, whether connected with particular business or otherwise—and there are not a few— are ignominious and deplorable. Both, however, deserve all they get ; the husband because he is, and of course must have been always, a fool ; the wife because she knew so little of the man before she married him, or perchance because she made a purely mercenary marriage. But notwithstanding the evils that are likely to attend such a reverse and unnatural state of affairs, *some* good will come generally : things might look blacker : worse would come unto that house, were the wife deficient *as well* as the husband ; worse would come unto the children.

Again, on the other hand, a woman should, whatever she do, look out for a manly man. She may admire and desire a lover before she really learns his deeper qualities, but if she get one who in the fulness of time manifests marked effeminacy, her love will wane, her admiration will sicken and die, and there will be a shakiness in their contract before long. A woman wants someone to lean on in times of weakness, someone to rely upon when

ADVICE TO SINGLE WOMEN

her own feminine force is spent, someone to look up to as a being that is in many ways mightier. A woman wants kindness, but firmness, sterling goodness, and strength in a man. She loves superior capacity and power.

When we understand that no two persons are alike, we know that this applies to brains as certainly as it does to anything. And, therefore, in order that married existence may be characterised by the truest and happiest harmony, the severest tax must be placed on the thinking or calculating powers of both. Natural temperament or disposition is one thing, and a controlling and guiding force of mind is entirely another. There are many of the married whose temperaments towards one another would be abominable were it not for the fact that repeated experiences have shown them the necessity of keeping down disorder by the strong reins of self-discipline. In such understanding lies the secret not only of knowing how to avert quarrels but to make-up peace and love again : when, prepared by the lessons of experience, the parties to a possible quarrel have learned to be careful, not only is a storm cloud seen looming early enough for the umbrellas of common sense to be got out, but the preventives of cool-

ness and forgiveness very quickly make
their appearance to make both happy once
again, and the rays of simple intelligence
soon make their way from both quarters
to brighten a situation fast developing into
an unpleasant state of affairs.

It is sensibility of the mind that averts
catastrophe, that turns on the hose to
a flame that would very soon be fanned
into fury, that clears away all the *débris*
of injured affection if by chance the battle
should have proceeded far enough, that
builds up again the fabric—perhaps a
better one than before. A temporary tiff
often ends with "We now love one
another better than ever." A still more
lasting love frequently follows a short
rupture.

Of all senses that contribute to the
happiness of a married life, nothing exceeds
that of duty. Whatever may be the
ordinary circumstances surrounding a pair
during life—there may be incompatibility
of temper, undue interference of the one
with the particular affairs of the other,
discrepancy in age, great difference in
health and thought—a fine sense of duty
will level both to a comfortable and
pleasant reasonableness. An understanding of simple duty will modify temper and
keep it within bounds; it will help the

recognition of a person's "own place";
it will fill in the difference of years and
make the experiences of each partner
blend happily; and it will also bring due
consideration for ill-health and weakness.

The financial aspects of matrimony are
very important; yet by some considered
far too important, and by others not
important enough, as the case may be.
Money is thought to be everything by
people who are sufficiently short-sighted
and selfish as to be swayed only by the
sparkle of gems and the parade of purple.
But what a rude awakening often lies in
store for these calculators! They have
hardly learned the A B C of life. The
greatest of earthly miseries may sit quietly
nestling under the softest and richest
raiment; criminal and demoniacal intent
may accompany envy, hatred, and malice,
each costly caparisoned. And on the
other side of the way may be contrasted
the prettiest picture of true happiness, clad
in quite humble attire; while instances
of pathetic charitableness and heartfelt
affection may often be found hand in hand
with undying regard and devotion, each
as full of health and joy as old clothes can
hold.

No; money should be more of a makeweight than it sometimes is; not the *only*

thing thrown into the balance of a heart. A full measure of strong and lasting love first, the money coming as a surprise afterwards, to make a gratifying certainty for the time to come; that should be the order.

If the makeweight of money can be put in on both sides, so much the better: "A just weight is his delight." Sometimes money is all on one side and virtues on the other. A fairly good balance may even be obtained, now and again, in this way, however, but nothing like so satisfactory a one.

Again, many marriages are contracted without any thought about money matters at all; nay, even in the face of the clearest poverty on both sides. They are young, generally, who go in for this kind of thing —sometimes very young, having more love than sense, more passion than calculation. Our fathers used to marry at twenty and twenty-one, and then look around for expenses afterwards. It was no uncommon thing for such young couples to hang around the parental larder by day and bag coals by moonlight. Then were the days of leavened bread; money was more plentiful at that time, and came for the waiting for, so to speak. Nowadays young men often reach twenty and still have to depend on their fathers' purses even for bread and clothing; they may even see thirty and yet go on carefully saving sixpences out of the washing and lunch allowances, in order to make just .a little pocket-money.

Between all thought and none, concerning money for marriage, there are various degrees commonly exercised. But the one that is best will be found somewhere about half way; since much money on one side and no money at all on either have both very good chances of bringing misery, something between the two is evidently the most desirable. There can be happiness for a time with very little money, it is true, but for what time? A month or more; or shall we say several months? If the state of a young couple could remain just as it is at the beginning of married life for an indefinite number of years, perhaps things would not turn out so badly on a small income; but a few months only may introduce a third, a child—and what then?

Marriages that are contracted simply for the sake of money or position are very often painfully unhappy ones. The balance of love, affection, passion, or call it what you will, may be perfect at first in these cases; but if it should wane, as it is *very* liable to, then awkward things are likely to happen. A husband with all the money can very easily say, if he is in a mood for quarrelling, " I took you without a halfpenny : where would you have been now if I had not married you?" Such remarks may be "thrown at" the wife. On the other hand, a woman with means who has married a man without, either because she thinks he will "come in for a lot," or because he *seems*—mark well the word—to be making a great deal, or, yet again, because—yes, even this—he has deliberately made her believe he has a lot, will afterwards be inclined to bully him for living on her means and for turning out such a fraud. Coolness and disappointment may thus arise, perhaps eventually leading to the occupation of separate rooms, if to no more.

One is bound to remember that there is often the cruellest, the most heartless, and sometimes positively criminal deception practised regarding "means" before marriage. A candidate for matrimony, of either sex, will sometimes be freely talked about as having "means," when the truth is that he or she has a few pounds per annum from some questionable investment. Designing and unscrupulous matchmakers' ears had better warm at this statement. And young men themselves are now and then given to masquerading as gallants of means. Instances have been known of small-salaried swells who have—perhaps quite early in an "understanding" or engagement—given out, to all who happened to be hopeful and interested, that they were "a member of the firm now," leading girls to suppose that their income and prospects were most satisfactory and promising, while they have really been second—or third—rate clerks. Such infamous rascals have swelled themselves out before their girls, and have excited envy and admiration so much, that when the time has drawn nigh for the nuptial knot to be tied they have not dared to give themselves away by retracting all that has been said during the billing and cooing stages. They have slyly crept into a lane with no turning, and have married, and the wretched truth has come out in painful dribblets as the earlier weeks of "making both ends meet" dragged on.

But there can be nothing more admirable and desirable than an alliance between a man of means and a woman of virtues, *provided* the man have some virtues too. His love will be constant and everlasting as he comes under the influence of those successive charms, attentions, and appreciations that are more to him than jewels and gold. And her own affection for him will live and increase as she admires his manly strength and ability, his capacity for bestowing comfort and happiness, his power of protection and creation.

SINGLE VERSUS *MARRIED LIFE*

WOMEN should not come to a hasty conclusion that marriage is the only satisfactory and really desirable goal to aim at. A more harmful and damaging notion could hardly take possession of the young idea. It is the means of producing self-consciousness and self-admiration, which often quite over-balance other very important attributes. It causes girls to pay far too much attention to themselves and not enough to other things, and encourages them to waste valuable time before the looking-glass that would better be occupied with some work judiciously calculated to improve their general capabilities and worth.

The one idea of looking nice and hunting for a suitor would be despicable if it were not so much done in sheer ignorance. It should be fully understood, once for all, that a woman looks her best, whether she be pretty in face and fine in form or not, when she is not thinking about herself, or when she is engaged in some kind of occupation that makes her forget herself and compels her to show that natural grace and unconscious exposition of beauty that is so conquering and irresistible to men. But the writer does not suppose for a moment that women will believe this all at once. They will not. Indeed, nothing seems sufficient to make them realise the truth of it. *Sometimes* men will see enhanced beauty in some "get-up' or artificial pose, it is true, but not men who are worth much. The man who falls in love with a powdered face and cannot see through a smile put on expressly for him, deserves all he gets if he goes on to the end, and is not much of a man, the reader may be sure. Women should therefore appreciate the simple fact that if they have any beauty at all, it will certainly show itself the best — the best for all purposes and ends, not for temporary or mere flirtation use, remember, but for all that is genuine, honest, and lasting—when the possessor is lost in realms of distant and independent thought.

A man will have but poor respect for a woman whose sole aim and effort is clearly seen to be directed towards making herself fascinating and "fetching" : he will first calculate that she must, in consequence of her methods, be so empty as to know very little else about anything ;

then he will come to the conclusion that she would, when married, have a double appearance to present to him, being "got up" and given to "putting-on" at one time, and rather untidy and plainly shabby at another. And, after all, what about the expenses of so much making-up and so many forced efforts to attract? Are they not rather heavy for some, and especially disappointing if the repeated and long sustained attempts are not altogether successful in the end? Are such things not dreamt of by men who are worth having? Do not a good many desirable male eligibles say to themselves : "The outward appearance is satisfactory enough ; her 'get-up' sets her off well, no doubt; but what about the bills for it all if I married her?" Women say, "How mean men are"; but the latter are apt to soliloquise, at this end of the century, "Not *worth* all the expense."

The best plan for women to adopt, therefore, is to aim for singleness if they wish to double themselves—whether with capabilities, riches, or marriage. And a single life is not so bad after all, even if it does go on to the end. By itself, and still more by the thought and expectation of it, it leads to useful occupation and healthy industry. Women must be doing something—at least the best representatives of them—and, if they are undistracted with the specious show and diligent effort of amorous intent, they will put life to some good and useful purpose, either with the simple idea of earning a living or for the better reason that their intelligence commands them to be up and active.

And, remember, there is absolutely nothing to equal work for maintaining a good state of health; that is, work of a suitable kind. Those who lead a life of idleness are the most miserable and unhealthy creatures on God's earth. They are generally so below par that doctor's tablets are daily bread to them; and, worse still, sometimes those tempting recipes of Bacchus are allowed to enter and administer their dangerous solace, annexing bit by bit, until a whole soul is consumed by the inroads of unrighteousness and *abandon*. Women drink as well as men, be it known, and nothing drives either sex more certainly to it than idleness.

The cultivation of good looks and idleness is apt to produce general dissatisfaction and ill-temper about almost everything else; and there is a limit, after all, to the attractiveness that may be attained by art and money. Pleasures do not last for ever; change as often as they may they begin to pall eventually. Therefore not only is a woman who is idle and only self-studious thus working out her own destruction, so to speak, she is planting seeds for a good deal of future unhappiness. But let her come to be clothed with a sense of duty, and the frills and feathers of her ignoble aspirations will soon grow less in importance; a better contentment will reign within her, and health will show itself more becomingly.

Girls who have nourished themselves and battened on hopes of marrying, and on very little else, sometimes live to encounter bitter disappointment. These are the ones who often have "to waste their sweetness on the desert air," languishing in convents or becoming miserable old maids. Out of temper with everyone and the world in general, they retire from it or grumble themselves into old age. Be careful of this, however: not all elderly single women are "miserable old maids." It is only those who have suffered from shattered hopes who develop into that particular species. Single women who have been industrious, and who have boldly carved out a career for themselves, can afford to snap their fingers at lost lovers, and thank the fate that at length designed them for a life of single success rather than the possible one of married misery, examples of which they will not be slow to find when in the mood.

The advantages of married life, and of single respectively, entirely depend upon the person—upon intelligence, energy, and temperament. The majority of human beings are certainly best married, if everything should point to the possibility of a satisfactory engagement being contracted with a view to this event. And it cannot be overlooked that some people are, in the ordinary meaning, eminently suitable for married life, while others are just the opposite.

If one take, by way of example, the case of some of our most distinguished men and women who have remained single, it would be seen that their life is one of much labour and application, that no state could have made it more so—certainly not the married one. It has been stated that a well-known man who was lately engaged with great success in moulding and fitting Africa for the English once replied, after being asked when he intended marrying, "I have no time for it; there is too much for me to do at the Cape at present." Now if such a man were married there cannot be a doubt that he would throw a good deal of his masterly energy into the up-bringing and career-carving of young sons and daughters, at the expense of so much that otherwise would be undividedly bestowed on matters concerning Empire making. His home would constitute a large section of his Rhodesia, so to speak, and occurrences within its four walls would detract from such concentration as would yield much mightier results outside.

A well-known commercial king is a single man, and has devoted his life to the development of a huge business concern made up of innumerable departments; had he been married, the anxieties and absorbing nature of paternal guardianship would no doubt have taken up a very great deal of the working powers that have built up his gigantic success. Yet some would no doubt argue that less millions and a wife with children would have been better for him; but this is not the point. In this chapter, and at this moment, the writer only asks for a consideration of the advantages of a single life, as compared with those of married, for those who wish to direct their minds towards great accomplishments. In a word, singleness permits of greater and more valuable concentration in work, and it avoids the innumerable little worries inseparable from parent-hood.

ADVICE TO SINGLE WOMEN

Examples could also be given of single women who have distinguished themselves, in certain spheres, to a greater degree than they would have done had they become wives and mothers.

One of the greatest advantages of married life to women is that it provides them with absorbing occupation, and rivets their mind on things that are in every sense natural, good, and elevating. Many girls are not so poor that they need work; others would be to some extent willing to work but cannot find anything exactly suitable, either because sedentary occupations do not agree with them or for some other reason. To such, then, married life, with all its little businesses and pleasures—especially when a family springs up—gives something for mind and body to devote themselves to throughout life—something to live for.

The advantages of a single life, on the other hand, also depend entirely upon the temperament of the individual. Those who have very great aspirations, who are for ever building upon former attainments, and who have never done seeking to accomplish great ends, such men and women get on very well single. They have really not the time; they do not permit themselves the opportunity; they will not allow their mind to wander amongst

amorous ideals, " to sport with Amyrillis in
the shade, or with the tangles of Nacera's
hair "; they are not exactly disposed to
substitute for business or nation-building,
a comparatively useless, weakly, and
playful dalliance ; they are far too business-
like to allow the poesy and sentiment surrounding sexual affection to get master of
them. In order to love properly and well
it is necessary to have plenty of time and
a favourable opportunity.

Those busy and hard-working women
who do not count so much upon the
advantages of marrying, but who deliberately and perseveringly make love to their
work, so to speak, and who have had such
earlier association with the opposite sex as
has taught them quite well what love is
and what courtship entails, what it is worth,
and what are the probable drawbacks to
an alliance for life—those are the ones
who would be likely to remain single
throughout life, were it not for the fact
that they so often present—provided they
have just sufficient personal attraction—
such a full measure of general inducement
to the opposite sex as is sure to secure
them, sooner or later, a handsome " offer "
which they cannot resist, and ought not to
resist. Experience is, after all, the thing
that teaches and guides, even if there be

ADVICE TO SINGLE WOMEN

ever so little of it ; experience of work and love also ; experience amongst those who have married and have had families, those who have provided ample instruction for any who cared and who were able to observe for themselves life's object - lessons ; experience in the sensation and the success of daily labour. Experience is the thing that fixes common sense and reliable reason permanently in the minds of those who have steps to take.

A single life is perhaps more suitable to men than to women in this respect : men earn more money in proportion to women, and they can therefore make things more comfortable for themselves in their life of bachelorhood ; while a large number of women of a similar station in life to such men, would undoubtedly be better off enjoying some satisfactorily espoused existence. There are exceptions, of course. Some women could never be thought very well off under marriage, if their health were constantly impaired in consequence, and if all real happiness were denied them, even if they should happen to have a rich husband ; such might easily be happier with ten shillings a week and board somewhere.

HOW TO FIND A HUSBAND

MOST of those who have married have no idea how they ever came to do such a thing; they could scarcely explain the commencement, or follow the stages through which they ascended the heights of nuptial bliss; neither could they correctly call to mind the forces or sensations which impelled them on their way.

A snake at the Zoo once swallowed another, unintentionally, having got hold of the large and lengthy mouthful by the merest accident — the very natural endeavour, while very hungry to extract a pigeon it saw protruding from the other's mouth! First it got hold of the pigeon, and after this the snake's head, and so on until the whole reptile was got down. The meal was continued either in sheer ignorance or through inadvertence; either it did not know how much was to follow, or it could not help itself, having got a start. It is not unlike this that a matrimonial partner is bitten at and swallowed. The bait may be mere paste, or a worm, or what not, but after a nibble it "takes," and then the helpless and frequently quite innocent struggle begins. Once a firm hold is obtained the whole lot has to be swallowed down, almost automatically, there being no drawing back. It is generally no use attempting to avoid taking the rest, the peristaltic process has begun and must go on until the tail end at length disappears. The machinery concerned in both human passionate affection and swallowing is, therefore, a good deal self-regulating : let it be merely started, it will tend to go on and on until the end.

Hence it will be seen that any thinking beforehand, any quiet and calm contemplation about what may happen, is quite out of the question in most instances of attraction that end in marriage. The snake had no idea that its fellow-creature would soon be drawn in, should it attempt simply to get the pigeon down, or it would not have begun the feed at all. So the majority of human beings, having made a start—yes, the majority—take the first kiss as their taste, and soon find themselves far on their way to the church, knowing not by what paths they arrived at this main one, and realising the impossibility of a return journey, no matter what may happen.

ADVICE TO SINGLE WOMEN

A study of long engagements is interesting. The parties concerned will often keep going on year after year without being able to bring their complaint to a head, as it were, and it is only by repeated attempts at breaking off that they realise with any certainty that anything has been on ; and so, quarrel by quarrel, bit by bit, path by path, they pick their steps to the altar. No-easy-way-back gives the strongest force forward,i n many an engagement to marry.

This is an age of education, a time for object-lessons and experience, when women read books and think more than they did formerly. There is now greater consideration for the morrow. But it must be candidly confessed that there is still a tremendous amount of interest shown, almost of necessity it would seem, regarding the simple question whether there is a chance of marriage or not with most women. Marriage is still looked upon as so much a calling that many women seem disposed to marry—*well* if they can, but to *marry*—somehow and something—at all costs, sacrifices, sufferings, and terminations, sooner than not. Is it well that this should be so ?

There are more men who marry because they cannot help it ; but many women do because they must. The long and short of it is, that passion places scales on the eyes of judgment, and therefore most men cannot *really* know what they are doing while in love ; but sex for sex there is less pure passion amongst women than men, for it is natural to the male of almost every order to show more of it than the female. Women are therefore compelled to a great extent to seek marriage merely in order to improve their lot in life. The reader must thoroughly realise this important difference.

Very often women are shamed into marrying ; they are reproached if they do not try. Mothers will not unfrequently tease and taunt, nay, even bully their daughters because they do not marry. Friends are also in the habit of chaffing girls who are not able to get engaged. " A good-looking girl like you ought to have been engaged long before this " is a very common form of banter. And there are some girls who have been so badgered at every turn by a host of female acquaintances—generally of the spinster, left-behind, and hopeless type, who are inwardly delighted that better-looking women than they are coming to the same state of things—that they have grown utterly desperate. Unbecoming and unlovely tempers have been thus developed, after a time, when the question has been painfully reiterated ; and it is not at all uncommon for one to hear expressions of the deepest disgust coming from the lips of the good-looking and disappointed, because no man has taken serious notice of them—while this has really been on account of their forbidding disposition.

Sometimes another rather remarkable development may be seen in those who have been subject to repeated failures. Girls who have tried hard, and *very* hard, for a long time will now and again begin to manifest, not a more ardent and fiery affection for the opposite sex, as one might think; not a further and bolder display of those higher educated gifts of fascination that have been improved by experience, but a subtle and sneaking hatred that shows itself like the dark side of a revolving lighthouse lamp—a few moments, and all is bright; but just as often comes darkness. There is this difference, however, that the light and darkness of the frequently disappointed heart do not remain quite evenly balanced for long. The moments of darkness generally grow longer, until at length, after hurling an everlasting anathema at perfidious and contemptible malehood, my lady slams the door of a convent in its face.

No; temper will certainly not do. Sweet, smiling resignation has a far better chance.

ADVICE TO SINGLE WOMEN

Temper is not attractive. There are girls to be loved, whom no man can resist. Take the one, for instance, whose eyes look far away—clean over the head of the speculative and mischievous little monster dancing his cloven attendance close by—in the direction of the *favourable* chances that little distant pictures on the horizon sometimes suggest. What eyes they are that look so! These are the women who conquer. Point out the man who is not attracted as by a magnet to that placid and lovely indifference which might be saying at the moment, "What I am I know not beyond what is told me; but such as I am let those admire who will; I shall not run after them and ask them; they ought to know their mind if they have one: if they have not they are worth nothing to me. If they admire, I smile, but only a very little, not enough to mislead them, but just so much as will make me attractive still." And where is the masculine heart that remains uninfluenced while a dainty figure sails past him—right past him, mind—fair to look upon, but unconscious of it, or *seemingly* so, and glides gaily away with gaze on anything far enough from *him*, as an angel that appears to have any other mission but matrimony, a goddess who has obviously some higher cause than flirtation.

ADVICE TO SINGLE WOMEN

This deliberate advice may be given to those who wish to marry. Appear as though you do not ; but mind you do it sweetly. Nothing is so fatal as a ticket stuck in a hat, on which is written : " I want to marry ; mother says I ought and must ; and I myself believe I really should do so, for more reasons than one." This will never do, because so many men think that the best things to be obtained in this world are those that are never advertised. Don't *say* you do not wish to marry ; that would be no good at all. But by every action, word, or deed make it *appear* that it is furthest from your intentions, and you will soon be happy. Do not look to see if anyone is gazing at you ; *think* they are, if you like, and put on whatever winning graces of face and form you think may be successful ; but, whatever you do, be careful that your thoughts are not read.

ADVICE TO SINGLE WOMEN

THE ART OF "MAKING-UP" AND ITS HYGIENE

WHO is there that walks this earth and is not "made-up" in some way or other? Young and old, savage and civilised—all try either to improve natural defects or acquired flaws. The pretty think they must polish, and even the aged are given to studying methods for the eradication of crows' feet. All do something. The aborigines cut themselves deeply in order to obtain desirable effects, and they do a good deal of painting and tattooing also. Some there are who mutilate themselves dreadfully: ears, lips, noses, and cheeks are deeply scored and furrowed with the knife. It may be interesting to observe that the only instances of absolute penetration of the flesh, for beauty or ugliness' sake, that still obtain amongst the British are ear-piercing, for the wearing of rings, and tattooing—if we leave out surgical plastic operations.

The British, therefore, exhibit few traces

of barbarity in their desire to make their
presence please, at least as regards mere
surface treatment.   They strike no further
than thin-skin deep as a rule.   Powders,
lotions, ointments, enamels, rouging compounds, skin tighteners, and such like, are
the kind of things chiefly made use of, and
abuse of, successfully and otherwise, for
the bare skin surface;   while wigs, pad-
dings, bustles, teeth, eyes, and sometimes
even noses and ears, are provided, in all
shades, in every amplitude and luxuriance,
and with an artistic moulding and accuracy
of outline that would do credit to the best
of sculptors.

Ought people to "make-up"?   Certainly
they ought.   It behoves every living being
to make the best of his or her appearance
—whatever they may imagine the best to
be—for the sake of art—for the sake of
having objects around that are pleasing to
the sight.   Our vision has a right to be
treated to anything and everything that
pleases it.   Notwithstanding all difficulties
that are liable to come in the way, everything possible should be done by each and
all to smarten up and show to advantage—
always keeping, however, within the strictly
reasonable.

Abuse of the methods of "making up"
there is always likely to be ; abuse of two

kinds, the one acting injuriously and the other unsuccessfully. It ought to go without saying that any processes of improvement that inflict injury to the skin or internal organs should be hunted out, exposed, and held up with strict warning. They may beautify, for a time, it is true; but later results must always be carefully taken into account. For instance, arsenic may improve the appearance of the skin in some people, and in certain quantities, while in other cases or doses it may produce the very opposite effect. The abuse that brings ill-success is one that properly concerns the visual sensibilities; it offends the truly artistic eye, and it sometimes does the opposite—often entirely unknown to the person cultivating it—to what was really intended: it frequently constitutes an amount of over-doing that may be abundant and even correct in theory, but wrong in *ensemble* and general effect. A hair-dye may sometimes be seen to have done its wonderful work to perfection through a looking-glass, for instance, but in the judgment of others it may look positively atrocious, and far too much of a golden hue, perhaps; while those undyed roots left on the side of the head, so well and often seen by others, may entirely escape the notice of the wearer.

ADVICE TO SINGLE WOMEN

Success or failure will depend to a very great extent upon the artistic idea of the experimenter, and upon the substance used, as may well be imagined. Notions concerning beauty are almost as varied as human features : what will be the acme to one may be absurd to another. The conceptions of different sets of people are generally very wide apart; yet, in due course, it will be frequently noticed that one class follows another in particular fashions. While servants will consider it "the thing" to arrange the bulk of their hair on one part of the head, ladies of West End drawing-rooms will at the same period be striving for fresh effect on quite another. Imitation by the lower classes is generally the signal for the production of a new style in the higher, to be set in Paris or Piccadilly. But each class is sure to faithfully follow another in time, once the highest has "set the pace." A game of paper-chase is played, as it were. The smart and designing hare chooses a certain new path as a leader of fashion, and the keen sighted hounds follow, after a time, some quickly and others dragging a long way behind. Rapid shop-girls run close behind fashionable ladies, naturally, and copy the higher styles the quickest, because they are in the way of learning them so well; 'Arriets and ten-pound-a-year domestics come in last with "the latest."

The champions of making-up, amongst amateurs, so to speak—those who operate on themselves, not making a living by touching-up others—are, of course, actresses. Their bread is not entirely earned by their skill in the art, but it of necessity depends partly upon it. They are bound to look their very best, whatever may have to be done to secure this ; and, working so much in companies, they are well able to procure such expert opinions, as regards result and material, from their friends, that their success is nearly always eminent from a stage-effect point of view. It is true that actresses often look comparatively unattractive, and sometimes almost ludicrous when seen off the stage. This may be due to one or two things : either they may be naturally so, and do not care to "make-up" for the street ; or they may adopt the same artificialities out of doors, or nearly the same, as they do on the stage ; and the latter would appear absurd, because the amount of touching-up necessary for the stage is so much greater and more exaggerated than any that could be well tolerated off it.

Here is a question for actresses : Is it better to look rather plain, but quite natural,

off the stage, and *not* be much noticed, or
to make-up to such an extent that people
do not see the defects underneath, but
simply and blankly stare. One would
think the former the more comfortable, or
at any rate the least trouble ; but the latter
will ever gain much favour from such per-
sonifications of vanity as could not live
without being looked at, somewhere, by
someone, or for something. An interesting
fact concerning the habits and ideas of
artistic and stagey celebrities—not quite
all—may sometimes be observed in such as
have come down in the world. The desire
to create admiration or wonderment is undying in them, whatever their reduced
circumstances may be ; they will stand on
their head in the roadway for applause, or
cut a throat to get paragraphed. Remember the murder of Terriss, and the intense
vanity of the criminal who committed it.

Let this warning be issued to the young
student of the art of self making-up. Mind
that the general health is not injured ; and
be careful lest the skin be damaged, or the
hair be made to come off, by the use of
advertised and fraudulent compounds. Let
the reader turn back to a former chapter,
to the advice given about quack drugs for
certain irregularities, and think for a
moment whether there is not a good deal

of the same nefarious spirit actuating the vendors of beautifying nostrums. It matters not which of these commodities is demanded, the retailers are screened, more or less, behind the very natural disinclination of the purchaser to make a fuss, or to go into a Court of Law after being cheated. The lower-class members of the hair-restoring fraternity know full well that their customers will never expose them before the public, for their own sakes. Hence the enormous amount of fraud and injury done to those who have a legitimate desire to improve their personal appearance. Young women should always act on the recommendation—personal, not written or advertised ; private, not picked up in shops —of trusty friends, and not be led away by " Thousands of testimonials."

One cannot condemn *all* the vendors of beauty-producing nostrums — of course not. There are some who are most reliable, fortunately.

Now let us look for a moment at what is commonly done to improve appearances. Take the hair first. Almost every colour in the rainbow can be produced by dyes, if necessary, but black, golden, light brown, or brown are the ones commonly chosen. Therefore after studying the advice already given concerning the quality of the stuff that is used, and concerning false advertised results, let the enthusiast be specially careful to get at the hair near the roots, as well as the rest, and not miss those little bits in front of the ears—often very small, but easily seen by the carefully observant. There are some who would scoff at the dyeing of hair; but it should be known that many men's and women's livings depend upon it; not only those who appear on platforms, but certain tradesmen and work-people are obliged to wear their hair a certain colour in order to obtain good work and command proper wages. Some are more or less compelled to look as young as possible. Grey-haired men are often refused work because they are thought too old for it, when perhaps in everything but hair they are quite young enough. Just this final advice may be given: women should mind that the colour they choose really suits them, or the hair will have D-Y-E printed on it, for every one to remark upon.

Wigs are useful, and it is often quite imperative to wear them. Women can lose their hair as well as men, and nothing so detracts from their charm. The wearing of fringes is also a most valuable method of beautifying a faulty head-covering; and some of the most perfect forehead adornments can now be purchased at a most reasonable price. It may be useful for wig-wearers to be reminded that sometimes such a colour and curl arrangement may be chosen as looks quite ridiculous. "When you are buying a wig, get a startler": this seems to be the notion actuating many a purchaser. The plainer and neutral tinted are, however, generally the better chosen.

Ladies are often pestered by hair-dressers who wish to sell certain dressings, regenerative balms, or hair renovators. Assistants have commissions on all bottles sold, and they become very persistent at the business. It is difficult for ladies to make an effectual reply when they are so bothered; but a very good answer for a man is that he *wishes* his hair to come off. That stops further importuning. A barber once kept on worrying one of his gentleman customers about suitable dressings and remedies for hair-falling-off. So after getting quite tired of it, the latter replied: "I am afraid none of your things are of the slightest use, because I *want* my hair to come off." The barber stared in blank astonishment. His hopes of sale were at once dashed to atoms. "My bald head," the gentleman continued, "is worth hundreds a year to me; I am young and a doctor, and I should not inspire half so much confidence amongst my patients if I did not look older." But it is feared that this tip for escaping barbers' balms is of no use to ladies, not even lady doctors.

That fatalities have occurred through the application of hair-dressings is common knowledge. Who does not remember the sad death of a lady whose hair caught fire, while being dressed, in a fashionable West End shop?

The face is a region of the body that lends itself most kindly to the artistic advantages of "touching-up." A little rouge, enamel, or powder—and there you are! Some pencilling to the eyebrows and darkening stuff for the lids, and there it comes! Beauty out of plainness. The thing is so easy.

Now there are one or two points about this touching-up of the face that are well worth referring to. It may be a dangerous practice for some women to adopt, however well it is done, because there is a certain class noted for it ; in fact, so much is this the case, that the individuals referred to are often recognised by their powdered faces alone. Therefore, more respectable women had better be careful that their powdering and rouging is borne discreetly, and with the accompaniment of scrupulous manners, or else they may be taken for somebody else.

"Touching-up" of the face must be done thoroughly well or not at all. Painted features ought properly to be indistinguishable, as an artificial production, to be of any real use. True art is to conceal art. But as often as not, or oftener, the artifice is easily seen, though the possessor may *think* otherwise. Girls have been known to go into a temper when accused of powdering, thinking that the truth could not possibly be detected; they have considered that strenuous denial is the only form of retaliation likely to successfully combat the accusation.

Then the necessity of always looking the same is also very great. Nothing will reveal little artificialities so well as different appearances of the face at different times; exactly the same tint should be studied, and it should merge beautifully into the fairer colour of the neck, without showing any unsightly boundary or unevenness. No; it is not easy to do well.

One cannot help coming to the conclusion that the game is not worth the powder, so to say, considering the trouble and risks it brings. And what anxiety there is in hot weather! Fancy having bee-lines of perspiration cutting sharp and easily-seen lines down the forehead and cheeks, probably just in the place, and at the moment, they can best be observed! There is one thing to be said in favour of hot weather, however: if this canal-cutting down the cheeks should by chance be remarked on, it is so nice to be able to say that powder has been used on account of the excessive heat—"To keep off sun apoplexy, you know. Sometimes people die of it. A little powder is *so* cooling."

Some girls have a practice which certainly deserves attention, and that is the dropping of solutions into their eyes in order to produce some sparkle or lustre that is supposed to be fascinating. Now surely this habit is not worth following! With the chances of injuring the sight or inflaming the delicate structures of the eye —and some harm is sure to follow in the long run—how much temporary good is done? Really extraordinarily little. What actress ever heard of a man falling in love with the brightness of her eye?

Again let women be warned. It is not one thing, but the deft and artistic arrangement of many points of attraction—the *ensemble*, in fact—that draws the fullest admiration. A girl once solutioned her eyes in such a manner that there was brightness, it is true, but such an amount of smarting followed that she looked as though she were suffering from some severe affection. Therefore, just as a graceful walk is preferable to small feet that are to a great extent made by tilted heels, and which are rarely seen, so is a natural and healthy appearance of the eyes better to look upon than any artificial and inflamed glassiness.

Happy are the young women who require neither powders, paints, nor pencils. They can afford to dress without show; they need not bother about pocket looking-glasses, nor worry on account of the heat. They can be kissed without hesitation— by their sisters or mothers—and need not have to run upstairs afterwards to see if any has come off.

Imagine a man, having received the reply in the affirmative that a girl has just given him, being branded with a wretched rouge mark on his face, and getting his black coat smothered, not by her embrace only, but by a good layer of whiting, or something, as well. Such things are not quite pleasant to think of, certainly.

The bust is an important section of anatomy to pay attention to. Those who are afflicted with a deficiency of nature's fulness must seek substance of some other kind. And here again a warning must be given against certain lotions or drugs that are advertised to restore "that natural profile so desirable to the sex." One of the reasons why these quack productions should be avoided is the same as that given concerning hair dressings and certain other compounds: the defrauded purchaser dare not complain, as it might ultimately bring some ridicule down upon her.

Padding is quite a legitimate procedure, though it might possibly be considered rather a cruel deception by some, and towards some. A good deal depends on circumstances. All women must allow that when a man loves and admires his *fiancée* for her many good points, not forgetting her beautiful figure, he must be a little disappointed when one day he finds all this beauty has had to be paid for in Regent Street, and only consists, for the most part, of so much cotton-wool, and other things. But, nevertheless, as has been laid down before, women are certainly entitled, nay advised, to make the best of themselves, and so no more need be said about it.

Those who suffer from deformities, such as curved spine or round shoulders, will derive much benefit from judicious and skilful padding; this goes without saying.

After all, good health is the best figure-former. Proper development is almost certain to follow regular, healthy living; and if a young woman be defective in figure let her proceed diligently to acquire a sound and vigorous state of health. She will derive more all-round benefit than patent medicines would give her, and will not have to pay so much for it.

One cannot reasonably find fault with dress improvers. They must be used strictly according as fashion dictates, however; and it is no use whatever going against this law-maker. They do not injure the health; there are no particular disadvantages arising from their use, and therefore they are entitled to be left alone by ill-natured critics. They make the contour of a woman more attractive and comely, according to the whim or fancy of the day, and all should be thankful.

Now the crinolines of old were dangerous. A child is remembered who had the sight of an eye destroyed through playing on the top of a bed where a crinoline had been placed. The steel of it snapped, and the sharp end pierced the eyeball. These awkward aids to beauty were also very troublesome to manage when in church, in carriages, or anywhere amidst a crowd; in fact, they could not be anything else but inconvenient at every turn.

ADVICE TO SINGLE WOMEN

The question of perfumes is a very vexed one. Some thoroughly believe in them; others cannot bear the mention of their name. A lady once remarked that she viewed everyone with suspicion who used scents; she always thought that such people had something to hide that was not quite agreeable; and was not this observant lady to some extent right in her surmise? Were one to ask the question, Should perfumes be used? The writer would answer Yes and no. If they can successfully neutralise anything objectionable, that cannot be completely got rid of by any ordinary or extraordinary means, then they are justifiable. But if a person be sweet, why make an attempt to be sweeter? Every one is more content to detect pleasant perfumes than any disagreeable ones, most certainly, but the sensation of purity and healthfulness that natural and neutral skins give off is far above all others, and quite priceless. Let the reader be advised that extreme cleanliness will accomplish a great deal, and give little necessity for artificial odours of any kind. Some chronic conditions of ill-health are hard to get rid of, no doubt; but perseverance with soap and water, and, still better, cleanly habits even *before* any chronic state has been reached, will bring their reward.

Health and cleanliness are better than all the perfumes of Araby.

The subject of ladies' clothing is one quite large enough for a book itself. Space will only permit rough reference to the different departments, however, and a glance will be given at underclothing first. Women should wear wool next the skin more than they do; thin in summer and thicker in winter. The plan of putting fine linen next the body throughout the year is one that has its dangers. Perspirations or exhalations given off from the body ought to have some material that will absorb them and allow them to find a free exit to the exterior. Linen soon gets wet and clammy, and persons wearing it will take cold more readily than those who wear flannel.

Corsets have already been referred to; but it may be further insisted that fairly loose articles of dress, throughout, are better than any tight ones. They may be made to fit the figure well enough, but should not be as tight as is sometimes found. A great feature of young woman's beauty is her suppleness, and there is something for the opposite sex to admire, in those finer feminine movements about the waist that denote a graceful and well-formed body underneath, beyond properly fitting clothes, certainly she ought not to convey to the observer any suggestion of being boxed up, or cased, as it were, allowing one no certain idea whether her interior is like that of a waxwork figure—shavings or sawdust—or something that is absolutely human.

Rational dress is all very well for those who fancy it. It allows freedom for the legs, and permits the addition of a top bar to the framework of a bicycle. Some think it hideous and improper. The former may judge rightly if the clothes are made in London and not in Paris, for as yet London tailors do not know how to cut rational dress: the latter opinion is likely to be held by those whose figures are so abnormal that they dare not risk anything beyond ordinary skirts. Whether a dress is proper or not very largely depends upon whether the eye is trained to it or not. Far fewer people are horrified at the sight of knickerbockers at the present moment than five years ago, for instance; and it is quite possible for a day to come when knickerbockers are scarcely noticed—if they should become commoner—everyone getting used to seeing them. It is rareness that causes attraction, or dissatisfaction, as the case may be.

The pessimistic need not frown and look

too serious about ladies' evening dress. Certainly the very *décolleté* designs are dangerous if the wearer be exposed to marked changes of temperature : common sense would tell us so. But all that is necessary for women to do, if they want to stop the mouths of medical complainers, is to carefully wrap up their shoulders and chest the moment they pass into colder air, whether in passages or out of doors. If ladies were to give the retort that doctors should take care that houses are built without draughts, and that the heating of them is arranged equally all over, upstairs and down, in passages and halls, as it is in some countries, they would give a good hit back that was fairly well deserved.

As to the healthfulness of hats, there is everything to be said in ladies' favour. They are far more hygienic than most men's, taking them throughout. One effect of very large and loose hats worn by ladies had better be mentioned, however : they have been found to cause spasms of the muscles of the neck—" trade " spasms, doctors call them. On account of swaying in the wind, or through want of proper fixture or balance, the head has been so habitually jerked, in order to bring the hat into position again, that certain movements of the neck have grown to be spasmodic and uncontrollable. Girls from 14 to 20 may often be seen jerking their heads to one side, in order to shift the position of a large feathery or flowery hat.

Ladies' boots are generally worn far too small, and with the heels of them too high. This complaint is not made unkindly or bad-temperedly: nothing of the kind. Small feet look pretty, of course; but if women have to resort to tilting up the heel in order to make their feet *appear* small, then the picture is not worth the pains. Why? Because high heels alter the style of walking, and prevent that ease and grace of movement that is far more entrancing to the other sex. Men rarely see women's feet unless they are really very large: they like a nice-shaped foot and ankle, it is true, but these will not be noticed before a comely and graceful gait, depend upon it. Young women should remember, once for all, that if they devote all their attention to their feet they will certainly detract, to a very great extent, from other points of beauty. Boots should comfortably fit the foot, and above all, allow graceful and easy walking; after that, if they are small all the better. The gait of an average Parisian is perfectly ridiculous: it is a stupid strut, a machine-like bobbing; all because the tiniest feet are considered by them to be a *sine quâ non :* up go their heels and a graceful gait is impossible.

How may boots affect the health? In this way : they can cause a great amount of suffering in the feet; corns, bunions, hammer-toes, or ingrowing toe-nails may form. Tight boots may also set up an aching about the ankle-joint, and indirectly lead to general illness; or further, they may help in producing disease, or in keeping it up, by limiting the power of exercise. Boots may also cause the ankle to give way or sprain severely, through the height of their heels.

How few women there are who have any faith in plain dressing, that is, for their own sex! They can see the virtue of simplicity of colour and design in the raiment of man, and, one and all, may give the opinion that "he *always* looks well in evening-dress"—an elementary arrangement in black and white—simple and always the same. But that is no matter. With many of the gentler sex quieter habiliments are the most becoming of all. How well the majority of hospital nurses look in plain dress and colouring, is the proverb and astonishment of everyone ; and it proves beyond a doubt that there are some people who can look well in the very simplest of dress. Many there are who do not look

ADVICE TO SINGLE WOMEN

well in anything, however; but, depend upon it, a good-looking girl, and a healthy one, dressed plainly, but sufficiently fashionably and well, is the prettiest sight of all—something for the eyes of gods and men.

> This above all—to thine own self be true;
> And it must follow, as the night the day,
> Thou canst not then be false to any man.
>   SHAKESPEARE.